ESSENTIAL SONGS FOR

tenor sax

Available for
FLUTE, CLARINET, ALTO SAX, TENOR SAX, TRUMPET,
HORN, TROMBONE, VIOLIN, VIOLA, CELLO

Note: The keys in this book do not match
the other wind instruments.

ISBN 978-1-4234-5534-9

HAL•LEONARD®
CORPORATION
7777 W. BLUEMOUND RD. P.O. BOX 13819 MILWAUKEE, WI 53213

Visit Hal Leonard Online at
www.halleonard.com

CONTENTS

ALL SHOOK UP

TENOR SAX

Words and Music by OTIS BLACKWELL
and ELVIS PRESLEY

ALL THE WAY

from THE JOKER IS WILD

TENOR SAX

Words by SAMMY CAHN
Music by JAMES VEN HEUSEN

AND I LOVE HER

TENOR SAX

Words and Music by JOHN LENNON
and PAUL McCARTNEY

ANYONE CAN WHISTLE

from ANYONE CAN WHISTLE

TENOR SAX

Words and Music by
STEPHEN SONDHEIM

Slowly and tenderly

AUTUMN LEAVES

TENOR SAX

English lyrics by JOHNNY MERCER
French lyrics by JACQUES PREVERT
Music by JOSEPH KOSMA

Slowly, with expression

BABY, I LOVE YOUR WAY

TENOR SAX

Words and Music by
PETER FRAMPTON

BACK AT ONE

TENOR SAX

Words and Music by
BRIAN McKNIGHT

BEAUTIFUL

TENOR SAX

Words and Music by
LINDA PERRY

BECAUSE OF YOU

TENOR SAX

Words and Music by KELLY CLARKSON,
DAVID HODGES and BEN MOODY

BENNIE AND THE JETS

TENOR SAX

Words and Music by ELTON JOHN
and BERNIE TAUPIN

Slow Rock

BLESS THE BROKEN ROAD

TENOR SAX

Words and Music by MARCUS HUMMON,
BOBBY BOYD and JEFF HANNA

D.S. al Coda

CODA

BORN FREE

from the Columbia Pictures' Release BORN FREE

Words by DON BLACK
Music by JOHN BARRY

TENOR SAX

BRING HIM HOME

from LES MISÉRABLES

TENOR SAX

Music by CLAUDE-MICHEL SCHÖNBERG
Lyrics by ALAIN BOUBLIL and HERBERT KRETZMER

Moderately slow

BREATHE

TENOR SAX

Words and Music by HOLLY LAMAR
and STEPHANIE BENTLEY

Moderately fast

BYE BYE LOVE

TENOR SAX

Words and Music by FELICE BRYANT
and BOUDLEAUX BRYANT

CALIFORNIA GIRLS

TENOR SAX

Words and Music by BRIAN WILSON
and MIKE LOVE

CAN YOU FEEL THE LOVE TONIGHT

from Walt Disney Pictures' THE LION KING

TENOR SAX

Music by ELTON JOHN
Lyrics by TIM RICE

Pop Ballad

THE CHICKEN DANCE

TENOR SAX

By TERRY RENDALL
and WERNER THOMAS

CLIMB EV'RY MOUNTAIN

from THE SOUND OF MUSIC

TENOR SAX

Lyrics by OSCAR HAMMERSTEIN II
Music by RICHARD RODGERS

CRAZY LITTLE THING CALLED LOVE

TENOR SAX

Words and Music by
FREDDIE MERCURY

COMPLICATED

TENOR SAX

Words and Music by AVRIL LAVIGNE,
LAUREN CHRISTY, SCOTT SPOCK
and GRAHAM EDWARDS

Moderate Pop

To Coda

CROCODILE ROCK

TENOR SAX

Words and Music by ELTON JOHN
and BERNIE TAUPIN

DANCING QUEEN

TENOR SAX

Words and Music by BENNY ANDERSSON,
BJORN ULVAEUS and STIG ANDERSON

Strong Rock

DON'T KNOW WHY

TENOR SAX

Words and Music by
JESSE HARRIS

DREAM LOVER

TENOR SAX

Words and Music by
BOBBY DARIN

DROPS OF JUPITER
(Tell Me)

TENOR SAX

Words and Music by PAT MONAHAN,
JIMMY STAFFORD, ROB HOTCHKISS,
CHARLIE COLIN and SCOTT UNDERWOOD

D.S. al Coda

CODA

DUST IN THE WIND

TENOR SAX

Words and Music by
KERRY LIVGREN

EASTER PARADE

from AS THOUSANDS CHEER

TENOR SAX

Words and Music by
IRVING BERLIN

Moderately

ENDLESS LOVE

TENOR SAX

Words and Music by
LIONEL RICHIE

FEVER

TENOR SAX

Words and Music by JOHN DAVENPORT
and EDDIE COOLEY

FIRE AND RAIN

TENOR SAX

Words and Music by
JAMES TAYLOR

THE FIRST CUT IS THE DEEPEST

TENOR SAX

Words and Music by
CAT STEVENS

THE FOOL ON THE HILL

TENOR SAX

Words and Music by JOHN LENNON
and PAUL McCARTNEY

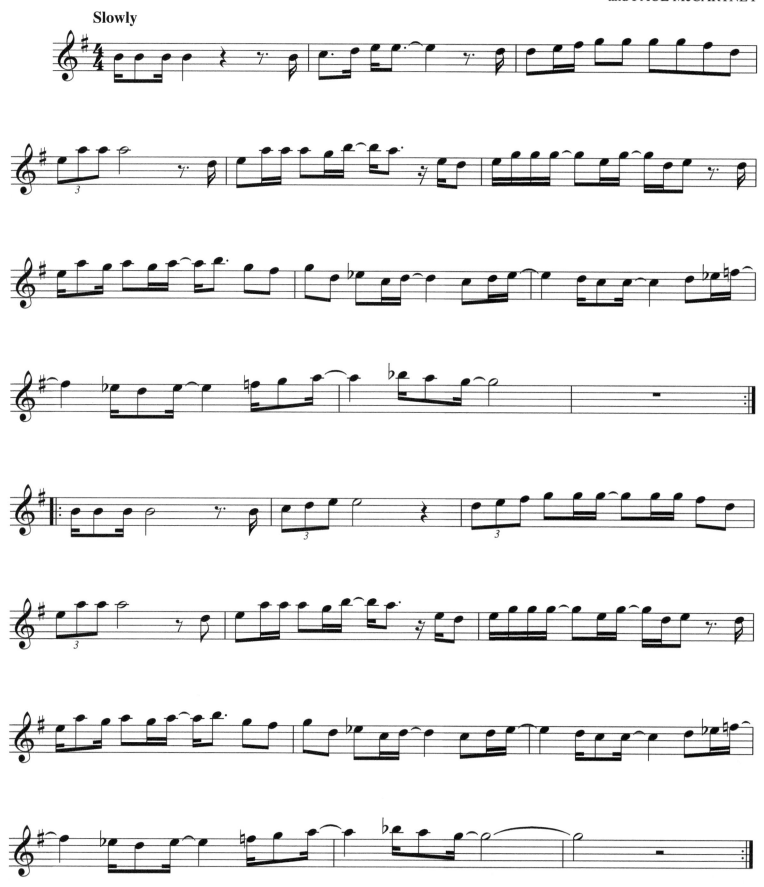

FOOTLOOSE
Theme from the Paramount Motion Picture FOOTLOOSE

TENOR SAX

Words by DEAN PITCHFORD
and KENNY LOGGINS
Music by KENNY LOGGINS

FROM A DISTANCE

TENOR SAX

Words and Music by
JULIE GOLD

GO AWAY, LITTLE GIRL

TENOR SAX

Words and Music by GERRY GOFFIN
and CAROLE KING

GOOD VIBRATIONS

TENOR SAX

Words and Music by BRIAN WILSON
and MIKE LOVE

GOT MY MIND SET ON YOU

TENOR SAX

Words and Music by
RUDY CLARK

A GROOVY KIND OF LOVE

TENOR SAX

Words and Music by TONI WINE
and CAROLE BAYER SAGER

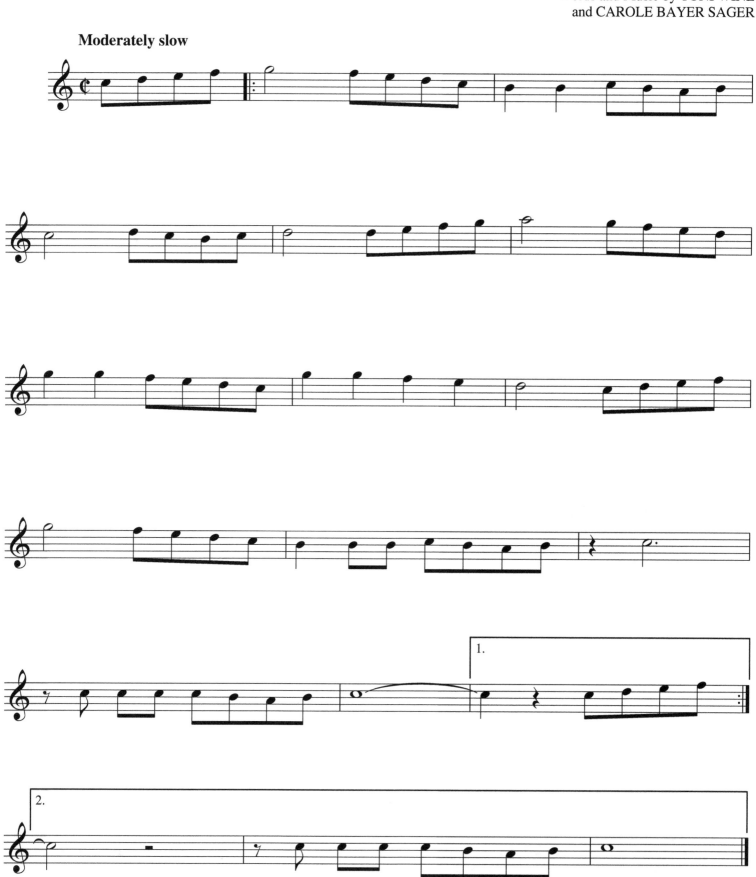

HAPPY TOGETHER

TENOR SAX

Words and Music by GARRY BONNER
and ALAN GORDON

HAPPY TRAILS

from the Television Series THE ROY ROGERS SHOW

TENOR SAX

Words and Music by
DALE EVANS

HEAVEN

TENOR SAX

Words and Music by BRYAN ADAMS
and JIM VALLANCE

HEAVEN

TENOR SAX

Words and Music by HENRY GARZA,
JOEY GARZA and RINGO GARZA

HELLO

TENOR SAX

Words and Music by
LIONEL RICHIE

HIGH HOPES

TENOR SAX

Words by SAMMY CAHN
Music by JAMES VAN HEUSEN

Moderately, with a beat

HOW CAN YOU MEND A BROKEN HEART

TENOR SAX

Words and Music by BARRY GIBB
and ROBIN GIBB

HOW SWEET IT IS (TO BE LOVED BY YOU)

TENOR SAX

Words and Music by EDWARD HOLLAND,
LAMONT DOZIER and BRIAN HOLLAND

I GOT YOU
(I Feel Good)

TENOR SAX

Words and Music by
JAMES BROWN

(Spoken:) Hey!

I HOPE YOU DANCE

TENOR SAX

Words and Music by TIA SILLERS
and MARK D. SANDERS

Moderately

I JUST CALLED TO SAY I LOVE YOU

TENOR SAX

Words and Music by
STEVIE WONDER

Moderately

I LEFT MY HEART IN SAN FRANCISCO

TENOR SAX

Words by DOUGLASS CROSS
Music by GEORGE CORY

I SHOT THE SHERIFF

TENOR SAX

Words and Music by
BOB MARLEY

Moderately slow, with a beat

I WANT TO HOLD YOUR HAND

TENOR SAX

Words and Music by JOHN LENNON
PAUL McCARTNEY

Moderately, with a beat

I'LL BE THERE

TENOR SAX

Words and Music by BERRY GORDY,
HAL DAVIS, WILLIE HUTCH
and BOB WEST

Moderately

I'LL BE

TENOR SAX

Words and Music by
EDWIN McCAIN

I'M WITH YOU

TENOR SAX

Words and Music by AVRIL LAVIGNE, LAUREN CHRISTY,
SCOTT SPOCK and GRAHAM EDWARDS

IF

TENOR SAX

Words and Music by
DAVID GATES

Moderately, with feeling

IF I HAD A HAMMER

(The Hammer Song)

TENOR SAX

Words and Music by LEE HAYS
and PETE SEEGER

THE IMPRESSION THAT I GET

TENOR SAX

Words and Music by DICKY BARRETT
and JOE GITTLEMAN

IN THE MOOD

TENOR SAX

By JOE GARLAND

IT'S A SMALL WORLD

from "it's a small world" at Disneyland Park and Magic Kingdom Park

TENOR SAX

Words and Music by RICHARD M. SHERMAN
and ROBERT B. SHERMAN

IT'S TOO LATE

TENOR SAX

Words and Music by CAROLE KING
and TONI STERN

Slowly

ITSY BITSY TEENIE WEENIE
YELLOW POLKADOT BIKINI

TENOR SAX

Words and Music by PAUL VANCE
and LEE POCKRISS

THEME FROM "JURASSIC PARK"

from the Universal Motion Picture JURASSIC PARK

TENOR SAX

Composed by
JOHN WILLIAMS

KING OF THE ROAD

TENOR SAX

Words and Music by
ROGER MILLER

LA BAMBA

TENOR SAX

By RITCHIE VALENS

LET IT BE

TENOR SAX

Words and Music by JOHN LENNON
PAUL McCARTNEY

LISTEN TO WHAT THE MAN SAID

TENOR SAX

Words and Music by
PAUL and LINDA McCARTNEY

Bright double-time feel

THE LOCO-MOTION

TENOR SAX

Words and Music by GERRY GOFFIN
and CAROLE KING

Moderately

LOUIE, LOUIE

TENOR SAX

Words and Music by
RICHARD BERRY

Moderate Rock

LOVE ME TENDER

TENOR SAX

Words and Music by ELVIS PRESLEY
and VERA MATSON

Moderately slow

LUCY IN THE SKY WITH DIAMONDS

TENOR SAX

Words and Music by JOHN LENNON
and PAUL McCARTNEY

MAMBO NO. 5
(A Little Bit Of...)

TENOR SAX

Original Music by DAMASO PEREZ PRADO
Words by LOU BEGA and ZIPPY

ME AND BOBBY McGEE

TENOR SAX

Words and Music by KRIS KRISTOFFERSON
and FRED FOSTER

A MOMENT LIKE THIS

TENOR SAX

Words and Music by JOHN REID
and JORGEN KJELL ELOFSSON

MY FAVORITE THINGS

from THE SOUND OF MUSIC

TENOR SAX

Lyrics by OSCAR HAMMERSTEIN II
Music by RICHARD RODGERS

Lively, with spirit

THE ODD COUPLE

Theme from the Paramount Picture THE ODD COUPLE
Theme from the Paramount Television Series THE ODD COUPLE

TENOR SAX

By NEAL HEFTI

ON TOP OF SPAGHETTI

TENOR SAX

Words and Music by
TOM GLAZER

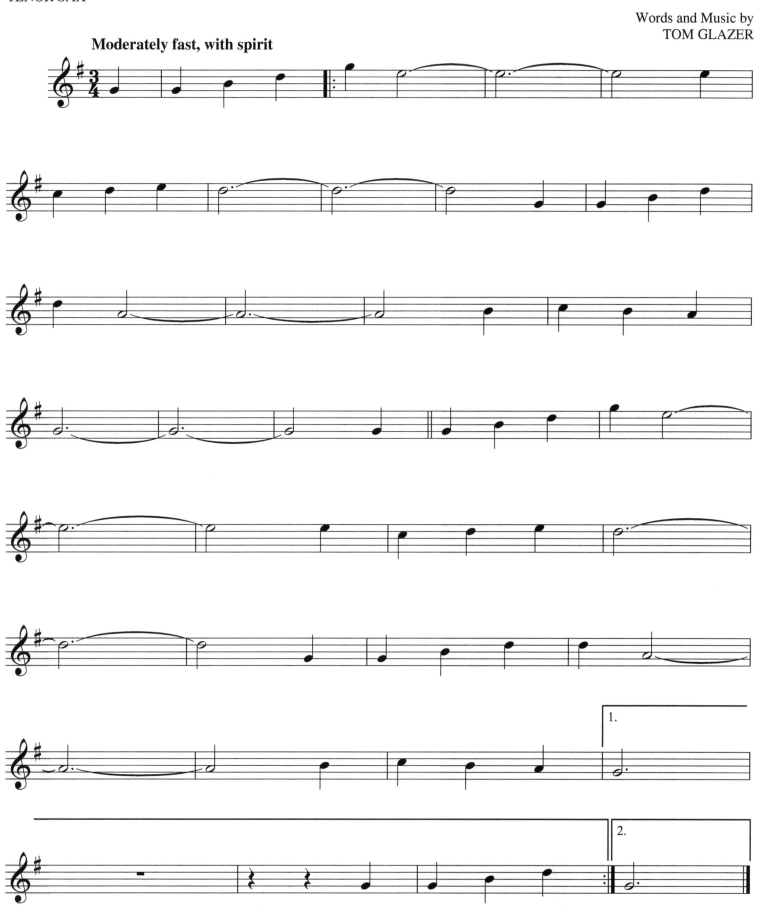

100 YEARS

TENOR SAX

Words and Music by
JOHN ONDRASIK

ONE NOTE SAMBA
(Samba de uma nota so)

TENOR SAX

Original Lyrics by NEWTON MENDONCA
English Lyrics by ANTONIO CARLOS JOBIM
Music by ANTONIO CARLOS JOBIM

PETER COTTONTAIL

TENOR SAX

Words and Music by STEVE NELSON
and JACK ROLLINS

Moderately

PUPPY LOVE

TENOR SAX

Words and Music by
PAUL ANKA

QUE SERA, SERA
(Whatever Will Be, Will Be)
from THE MAN WHO KNEW TOO MUCH

TENOR SAX

Words and Music by JAY LIVINGSTON
and RAY EVANS

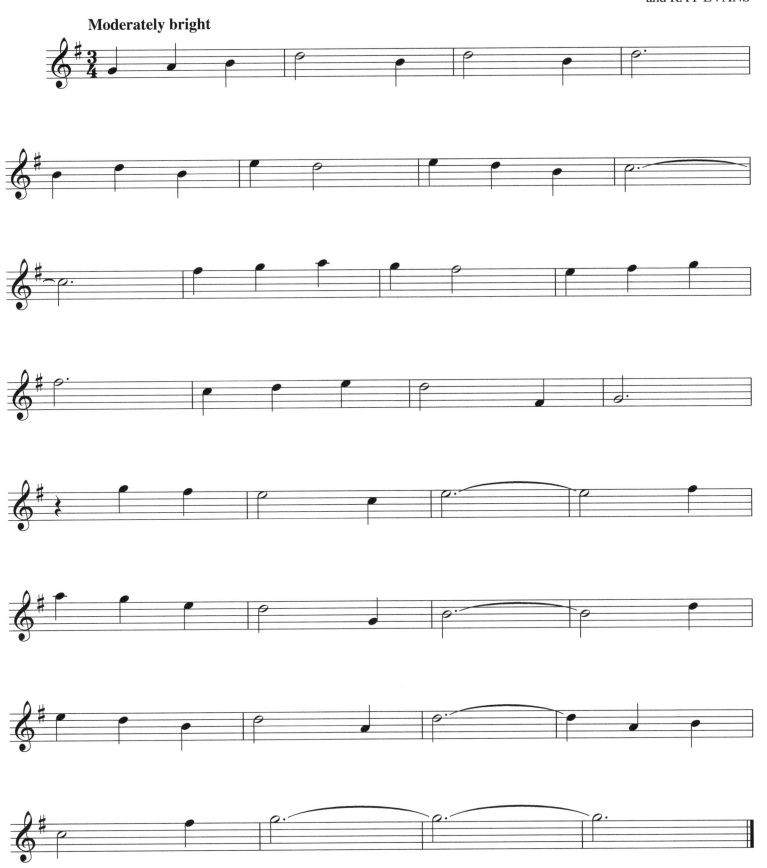

R.O.C.K. IN THE U.S.A
(A Salute to 60's Rock)

TENOR SAX

Words and Music by
JOHN MELLENCAMP

Fast Rock

THE RAINBOW CONNECTION

from THE MUPPET MOVIE

TENOR SAX

Words and Music by PAUL WILLIAMS
and KENNETH L. ASCHER

RAINDROPS KEEP FALLIN' ON MY HEAD

from BUTCH CASSIDY AND THE SUNDANCE KID

TENOR SAX

Lyric by HAL DAVID
Music by BURT BACHARACH

ROCKIN' ROBIN

TENOR SAX

Words and Music by
J. THOMAS

SAILING

TENOR SAX

Words and Music by
CHRISTOPHER CROSS

Moderately

SEE YOU LATER, ALLIGATOR

TENOR SAX

Words and Music by
ROBERT GUIDRY

SEVENTY SIX TROMBONES
from Meredith Willson's THE MUSIC MAN

TENOR SAX

By MEREDITH WILLSON

March tempo

SHAKE, RATTLE AND ROLL

TENOR SAX

Words and Music by
CHARLES CALHOUN

SHOUT

TENOR SAX

Words and Music by ROLAND ORZABAL
and IAN STANLEY

Moderately, with a beat

Fine

D.C. al Fine

SIXTEEN GOING ON SEVENTEEN

from THE SOUND OF MUSIC

TENOR SAX

Lyrics by OSCAR HAMMERSTEIN II
Music by RICHARD RODGERS

SMOOTH

TENOR SAX

Words by ROB THOMAS
Music by ROB THOMAS and ITALL SHUR

SO NICE
(Summer Samba)

TENOR SAX

Original Words and Music by MARCOS VALLE
and PAULO SERGIO VALLE
English Words by NORMAN GIMBEL

THE SOUND OF MUSIC

from THE SOUND OF MUSIC

TENOR SAX

Lyrics by OSCAR HAMMERSTEIN II
Music by RICHARD RODGERS

SPINNING WHEEL

TENOR SAX

Words and Music by
DAVID CLAYTON THOMAS

Funky, moderate Rock

SPLISH SPLASH

TENOR SAX

Words and Music by BOBBY DARIN
and MURRAY KAUFMAN

STAND BY ME

TENOR SAX

Words and Music by JERRY LEIBER,
MIKE STOLLER and BEN E. KING

SUNNY

TENOR SAX

Words and Music by
BOBBY HEBB

Moderate Rock

SUPERCALIFRAGILISTICEXPIALIDOCIOUS

from Walt Disney's MARY POPPINS

TENOR SAX

Words and Music by RICHARD M. SHERMAN
and ROBERT B. SHERMAN

SURFIN' U.S.A.

TENOR SAX

Words and Music by
CHUCK BERRY

TAKIN' CARE OF BUSINESS

TENOR SAX

Words and Music by
RANDY BACHMAN

Moderate Rock

TEARS IN HEAVEN

TENOR SAX

Words and Music by ERIC CLAPTON
and WILL JENNINGS

TENNESSEE WALTZ

TENOR SAX

Words and Music by REDD STEWART
and PEE WEE KING

THAT'LL BE THE DAY

TENOR SAX

Words and Music by JERRY ALLISON,
NORMAN PETTY and BUDDY HOLLY

THIS LOVE

TENOR SAX

Words and Music by ADAM LEVINE
and JESSE CARMICHAEL

TIE A YELLOW RIBBON
ROUND THE OLE OAK TREE

TENOR SAX

Words and Music by L. RUSSELL BROWN
and IRWIN LEVINE

Moderately bright

TIJUANA TAXI

TENOR SAX

Words by JOHNNY FLAMINGO
Music by ERVAN "BUD" COLEMAN

Moderately

TRUE COLORS

TENOR SAX

Words and Music by BILLY STEINBERG
and TOM KELLY

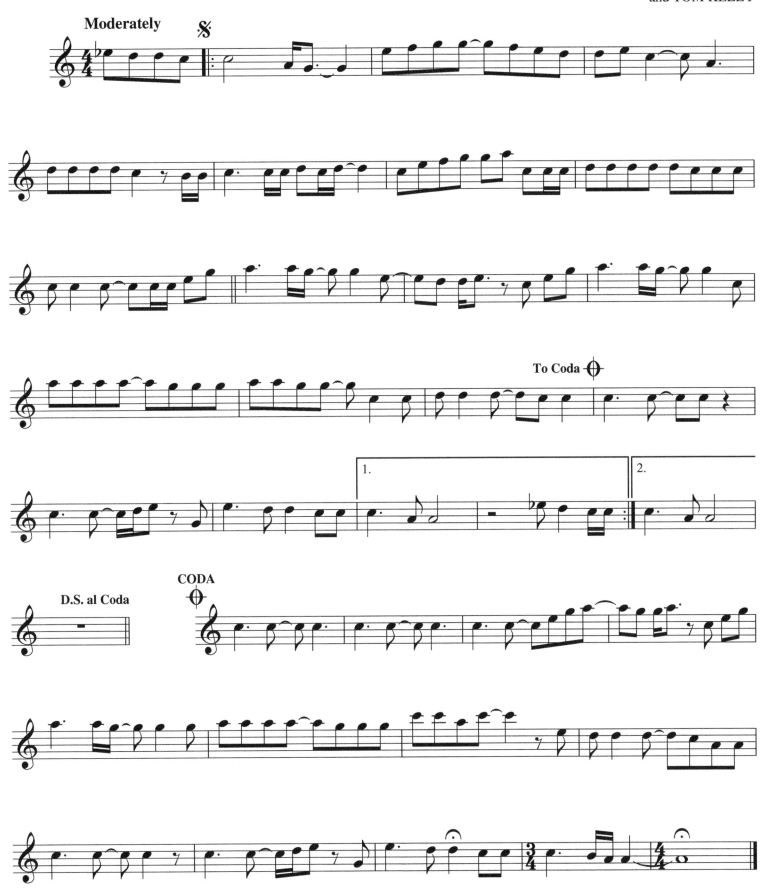

THE TWIST

TENOR SAX

Words and Music by
HANK BALLARD

UP WHERE WE BELONG

from the Paramount Picture AN OFFICER AND A GENTLEMAN

TENOR SAX

Words by WILL JENNINGS
Music by BUFFY SAINTE-MARIE and JACK NITZSCHE

WALKING IN MEMPHIS

TENOR SAX

Words and Music by
MARC COHN

THE WAY YOU LOOK TONIGHT

from SWING TIME

TENOR SAX

Words by DOROTHY FIELDS
Music by JEROME KERN

WE ARE FAMILY

TENOR SAX

Words and Music by NILE RODGERS
and BERNARD EDWARDS

WE ARE THE CHAMPIONS

TENOR SAX

Words and Music by
FREDDIE MERCURY

Moderately slow

WE BUILT THIS CITY

TENOR SAX

Words and Music by BERNIE TAUPIN, MARTIN PAGE,
DENNIS LAMBERT and PETER WOLF

WE'VE ONLY JUST BEGUN

TENOR SAX

Words and Music by ROGER NICHOLS
and PAUL WILLIAMS

WHITE FLAG

TENOR SAX

Words and Music by RICK NOWELS,
ROLLO ARMSTRONG and DIDO ARMSTRONG

A WHOLE NEW WORLD
from Walt Disney's ALADDIN

TENOR SAX

Music by ALAN MENKEN
Lyrics by TIM RICE

Y.M.C.A.

TENOR SAX

Words and Music by JACQUES MORALI,
HENRI BELOLO and VICTOR WILLIS

YESTERDAY

TENOR SAX

Words and Music by JOHN LENNON
and PAUL McCARTNEY

YOU ARE MY SUNSHINE

TENOR SAX

Words and Music by
JIMMIE DAVIS

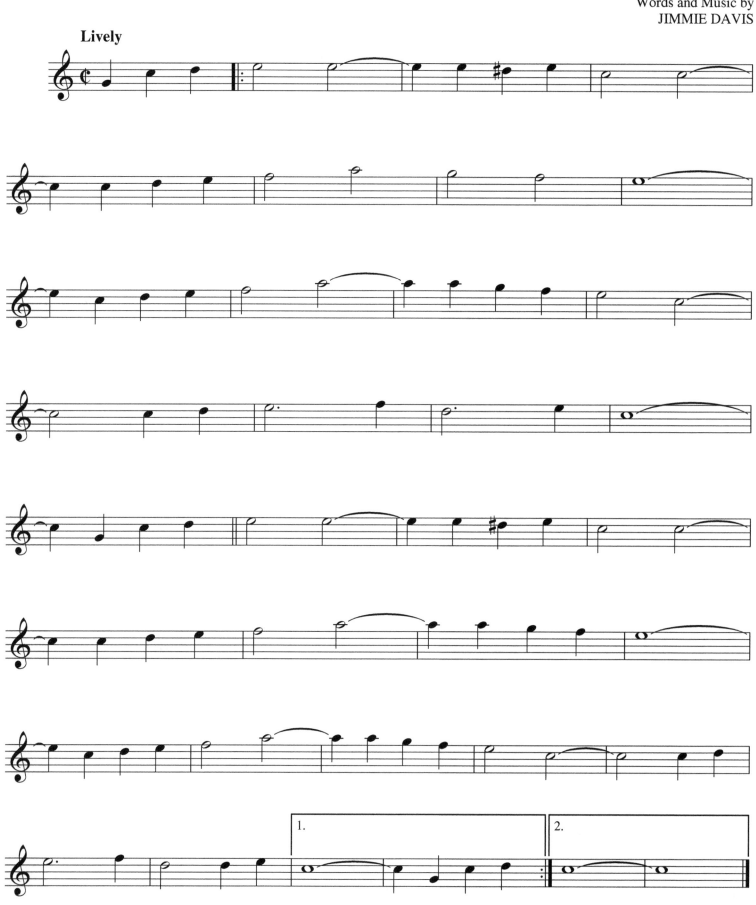

YOU LIGHT UP MY LIFE

TENOR SAX

Words and Music by
JOSEPH BROOKS

Moderately slow

YOU ARE THE MUSIC IN ME

from the Disney Channel Original Movie HIGH SCHOOL MUSICAL 2

TENOR SAX

Words and Music by
JAMIE HOUSTON

Moderately fast Rock

YOU'RE BEAUTIFUL

TENOR SAX

Words and Music by JAMES BLUNT,
SACHA SKARBEK and AMANDA GHOST

YOU'RE STILL THE ONE

Tenor Sax

Words and Music by SHANIA TWAIN
and ROBERT JOHN LANGE

YOU'VE GOT A FRIEND IN ME

from Walt Disney's TOY STORY

TENOR SAX

Music and Lyrics by
RANDY NEWMAN

YOUR SONG

TENOR SAX

Words and Music by ELTON JOHN
and BERNIE TAUPIN

ZOOT SUIT RIOT

TENOR SAX

Words and Music by
STEVE PERRY